Flightmares

Sky-High Humor

Robert D. Reed, Ph.D. WKF
White Knuckle Flier

Robert D. Reed Publishers

Robert D. Reed Publishers • Bandon, OR

Cartoons are available for reprinting. Write for fees and
permissions.

Robert D. Reed Publishers
P.O. Box 1992
Bandon, OR 97411
Phone: 541-347-9882; Fax: -9883
E-mail:4bobreed@msn.com
Website:www.rdrpublishers.com

Editor: Cleone Reed
Cover Designer: Cleone Reed
Photo Collages: Cleone Reed
Cartoonist: Khairul Izzuddin
e-Book Designer: Susan Leonard

Soft cover ISBN: 978-1-944297-16-9
eBook ISBN: 978-1-944297-17-6

Library of Congress Number: 2017902694

Designed, Formatted, and Printed in the United States of America

Dedication

Dedicated to my favorite partner,
my wife Cleone,
in or out of my seat,
in stormy weather or smooth flying.
The one who holds my hand
during any flying conditions.
Helps me find my seat
even when my eyes are full of tears
or shut out of fear.
And books all our seats on planes that
NEVER GO DOWN.

Acknowledgments

First I want to acknowledge
my darling wife Cleone
who helps me with all my needs
of writing and publishing.
No matter how bad I do,
she always makes me look better.

Thanks go to my friend
Malcolm Kushner,
America's Favorite Humor Consultant
and author of several books
I have published,
for writing the Foreword.

I want to thank the
cartoonist from Malaysia,
Khairal Izzuddin.
for creating cartoons
to visually showcase my ideas.

Appreciation goes to my departed friend
Danek Kaus,
for his contributions and support for this book
before he died.

I appreciate my brother Harry
who can't swim
so he never flies over water
but always laughs at my jokes.

And to my children and grandchildren,
you may purchase this book
at a very generous discount!
(No refunds please!)

Table of Contents

Who invented
the first airplane
that didn't fly?

The Wrong Brothers

Foreword to Flightmares

By Malcolm Kushner

"If God had wanted us to fly,
He would have given us wings."

That was a common refrain in the 20th century
as airplanes grew from a novelty into a major
form of commercial transportation. It was also a
great way to cover-up a fear of flying by appear-
ing to be a devout person of faith.

Now, more than a hundred years since the
invention of flying machines, you don't hear
the "wings" excuse any more. Flying has been
accepted as a scientific achievement, and it's
viewed as perfectly natural. But many people are
still scared of it. So what can they do?

First, they can come up with a new excuse!

If God had wanted us to fly, He would not have:

✈ Put a safety card located in the seat pocket in front of you.

✈ Put emergency exits on the aircraft in the front, in the back, and over the wings.

✈ Equipped each exit with a safety slide that can be detached and used as a flotation device.

✈ Located an individual life vest in a pouch beneath your seat.

✈ Equipped the aircraft with aisle path lighting which is located on the floor in the left and right aisles should cabin visibility be impaired.

✈ Provided yellow oxygen masks that deploy from the ceiling compartment located above you in case there is a loss in cabin pressure

✈ Allowed your electronic devices to interfere with the aircraft's navigational and communication systems.

✈ Asked that you keep your seatbelt fastened while seated in case we experience some unexpected turbulence.

But don't worry. **Flightmares** addresses all these concerns and more in a way that will have you smiling throughout your flight. So make sure your seat belts are fastened, secure your tray tables into their full upright and locked position, and get ready to laugh.

Q: Why don't ducks
tell jokes when they fly?

A: Because they would quack up!

Introduction

After publishing 2000 books over my career, I have a desire to have a lighter side of me shown in this book.

Many of the books I have published were of more serious subjects, which I am proud to have done and continue to do. If you are interested in my last few years of titles, visit my web site at www.rdrpublishers.com.

Enjoy the research on Sky-High Humor that friends and I have gathered; and especially enjoy the many cartoons I contracted with a Malaysian cartoonist, Khairal Izzuddin.

I always welcome comments and other jokes and stories which can be added into new editions of Flightmares.

Flying

is the second
greatest thrill
known to man...

Landing

is the first!

Chapter One

THE LOVE OF FLYING

Lovers of air travel find it exhilarating to hang poised between the illusion of immortality and the fact of death.

> ~ Alexander Chase, "Perspectives," 1966

How strange is this combination of proximity and separation? That ground—seconds away—thousands of miles away.

> ~ Charles A. Lindbergh

Flight is the only truly new sensation than men have achieved in modern history.

> ~ James Dickey

The butterfly is a flying flower. . .

~ Ponce Denis Écouchard Lebrun

More than anything else the sensation is one of perfect peace mingled with an excitement that strains every nerve to the utmost, if you can conceive of such a combination.

~Wilbur Wright

The modern airplane creates a new geographical dimension. A navigable ocean of air blankets the whole surface of the globe. There are no distant places any longer: the world is small and the world is one.

~ Wendell Willkie

Within all of us is a varying amount of space lint and star dust, the residue from our creation. Most are too busy to notice it, and it is stronger in some than others. It is strongest in those of us who fly and is responsible for an unconscious, subtle desire to slip into some wings and try for the elusive boundaries of our origin.

~ K.O. Eckland, "Footprints on Clouds"

The bluebird carries the sky on his back.

~ Henry David Thoreau

When once you have tasted flight, you will for-
ever walk the earth with your eyes turned sky-
ward, for there you have been, and there you will
always long to return.

~ Leonardo Da Vinci

You haven't seen a tree until you've seen its
shadow from the sky.

~ Amelia Earhart

Once you have learned to fly your plane, it is far
less fatiguing to fly than it is to drive a car. You
don't have to watch every second for cats, dogs,
children, lights, road signs, ladies with baby car-
riages, and citizens who drive out in the middle
of the block against the lights. . . . Nobody who
has not been up in the sky on a glorious morning
can possibly imagine the way a pilot feels in free
heaven.

~ William T. Piper

The desire to reach for the sky runs deep in our human psyche.

~ Cesar Pelli

Why fly? Simple. I'm not happy unless there's some room between me and the ground.

~ Richard Bach

The Wright Brothers created the single greatest cultural force since the invention of writing. The airplane became the first World Wide Web, bringing people, languages, ideas, and values together.

~ Bill Gates

If happy little bluebirds fly beyond the rainbow, why oh why can't I?

~ E.Y. Harburg

I pick the prettiest part of the sky and I melt into the wing and then into the air, till I'm just soul on a sunbeam.

~ Richard Bach

The desire to fly is an idea handed down to us by our ancestors who, in their grueling travels across trackless lands in prehistoric times, looked enviously on the birds soaring freely through space, at full speed, above all obstacles, on the infinite highway of the air.

~ Wilbur Wright

Pilots are a rare kind of human. They leave the ordinary surface of the word, to purify their soul in the sky, and they come down to earth, only after receiving the communion of the infinite.

~ Jose Maria Velasco Ibarra

Given angel's wings, where might you fly?
In what sweet heaven might you find your love?
Unwilling to be bound, where might you move,
Lost between the wonder and the why?. . .

~ Nicholas Gordon

Spread your wings and let the fairy in you fly!

~ Author Unknown

Chapter Two

THE FEAR OF FLYING

Fear of flying is a fear of being on an airplane (aeroplane), or another flying vehicle, such as a helicopter, while in flight. It is also referred to as a flying phobia, flight phobia, aviophobia, or aerophobia (although the last also means a fear of drafts or of fresh air.)

Fear of flying may be a distinct phobia in itself, or it may be an indirect combination of one or more other disorders, such as claustrophobia (a phobia of being restricted, confined, or unable to escape) or acrophobia (anxiety or dread of being at a great height). It may have other causes as well, such as agoraphobia (especially the type associated with having a panic attack in a place they can't escape from).

~ Wikipedia

Statistics

Nearly 1 in 3 adult Americans is either anxious about flying (18.1%) or afraid to fly (12.6%).

Of those afraid to fly:
- ✈ 73% were fearful of mechanical problems during flight.
- ✈ 62% were afraid of being on a flight during bad weather.
- ✈ 36% were afraid of mechanical problems on the ground.
- ✈ 36% were afraid about flying at night.
- ✈ 33% feared flying over a body of water.

There is a 1 in 11 million chance of being involved in an airplane accident and 96% of passengers survive airline accidents.

From the years 2002–2007, there were 109 deaths due to plane crashes and 196,724 due to car accidents.

Across the globe, 3 million passengers fly on any given day, and 1.8 million of these are flights in the United States, on a total of 24,600 flights.

www.flyfright.com/statistics

Political ambitions finally trumped Ronald Regan's fear of flying. But in response to someone saying he must have overcome his phobia of flying, he said:

Overcome it, hell.
I'm holding this plane up
in the air
by sheer willpower

~ Ronald Reagan

I don't like flying because I'm afraid of crashing into a large mountain. I don't think Dramamine is going to help.

~ *Kaffie*, in the 1992 movie *A Few Good Men*

My fear of flying starts as soon as I buckle myself in and then the guy up front mumbles a few unintelligible words then before I know it I'm thrust into the back of my seat by acceleration that seems way too fast and the rest of the trip is an endless nightmare of turbulence, of near misses. And then the cabbie drops me off at the airport.

~ Dennis Miller

I don't have a fear of flying; I have a fear of crashing.

~ Billy Bob Thornton

I was always afraid of dying. Always. It was my fear that made me learn everything I could about my airplane and my emergency equipment, and kept me flying respectful of my machine and always alert in the cockpit.

~ Chuck Yeager

I feel about airplanes the way I feel about diets. It seems to me that they are wonderful things for other people to go on.

~ Jean Kerr, "Mirror, Mirror, on the Wall,"
The Snake Has All the Lines, 1958

I took a Fear of Flying class, and I always missed the class, because I was always flying.

~ Sara Blakely

As with most phobias, the fear of flying does make some sense, but if ever there was a fear worth quashing then this is it. After all, life is short, and there's a great big world to explore out there.

~ Beth Ditto

The only thing that scares me about flying is the drive to the airport

It is far better to arrive late in this world than early in the next.

A RIDDLE

A man hijacks a plane and asks for two parachutes from the officials. He jumps off the plane with one parachute and left the other one behind. Why did he ask for two parachutes?

If the officials thought he was jumping with a hostage, they would never risk giving him a faulty parachute.

Chapter Three

LUGGAGE

Too Stuffed?

Try putting this one in an overhead bin!

https://www.pinterest.com/pin/348747564870435354/

"Why is the mistletoe hanging over the baggage counter?" asked the airline passenger, amid the holiday rush.

The clerk replied, "It's so you can kiss your luggage good-bye."

Luggage Stickers to assure no one will mistake yours for theirs!

LUGGAGE TAGS

goofy:
crazy, stupid, silly
(as in: you will look goofy in my clothes)

take my luggage
do my laundry

you won't look good
in my clothes

please don't take
my bag
i'm too old to chase you

not worth taking

I Dare You to Try
to Steal My Bag!

Too Much Luggage?

This is too much luggage for one person!

Too Big?

Just a little over fifty pounds!

Photo by Dana Edelson, 2013 NBC

According to the Bureau of Transportation Statistics (http://www.transtats.bts.gov/), a total of 631,939,829 passengers boarded domestic flights in the United States in the year 2010. This averages to **1.73 million passenger** flying per day. No wonder my luggage gets lost.

He was worried that the airline might lose his bag with all the sausages he bought during his trip to Germany. That would be the *wurst case scenario.*

He had his luggage torn to pieces, so he asked his lawyer if he could sue the airline. He said, "You don't have much of a case."

There was an incident at the airport when a large collection of suitcases fell over in the luggage area. Experts suspect it was *pile it error.*

The scientific theory I like best is that the rings of Saturn are composed entirely of lost airline luggage.
~ Mark Russell

At an airport, one of my friends suggested we disguise ourselves as luggage. I said, "Let's not get carried away."

A passenger piled his luggage on the scale at an airline counter in New York and said to the ticket agent: "I'm flying to Los Angeles. I want the large bag sent to Denver and the two small ones to Cincinnati."

"I'm sorry sir, but we can't do that," said the ticket agent.

"That's good to hear because that's where they ended up the last time I flew this route."

A Good idea??

Traveling with Twins. Cultura RM/Emma Kim/Getty Images

NO! TRUE STORIES:
People Who Tried Got Caught!

Turned over to authorities in Paris upon arrival:

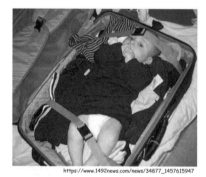

https://www.1492news.com/news/34877_1457615947

Caught in x-ray scan going through security:

http://www.nydailynews.com/news/world/x-ray-scan-reveals-
smuggled-boy-suitcase-article-1.2215202

I used to think that nails-down-a-chalkboard was the worst sound in the world. Then I moved on to people-eating-cereal-on-the-phone. But only this week did I stumble across the rightful winner: it's the sound of a baggage carousel coming to a grinding halt, having reunited every passenger on your flight with their luggage, except for you.

~ Sloane Crosley

A friend got arrested after covering some luggage in oil. They dropped the case.

The engine
is the heart
of an airplane,
but the pilot
is its soul.

~ Walter Raleigh

Chapter Four

PILOTS

Pilots in flight training

© 2017 Robert D. Reed

There are old pilots, and there are bold pilots,
but there are no old bold pilots.

Pilots are just plane people with a special air about them.

A plane was taking off from Kennedy Airport. After it reached a comfortable cruising altitude the Captain made an announcement over the intercom, "Ladies and Gentlemen, this is your captain speaking. Welcome to Flight Number 293, nonstop from New York to Los Angeles. The weather ahead is good and, therefore, we should have a smooth and uneventful flight. Now sit back and relax . . .

"OH, MY GOD!"

Silence followed, and after a few minutes, the captain came back on the intercom and said, "Ladies and Gentlemen, I am so sorry if I scared you earlier. While I was talking to you, the flight attendant accidentally spilled a cup of hot coffee in my lap. You should see the front of my pants!"

A passenger in Coach yelled, "That's nothing. You should see the back of mine!"

If you see a pilot who looks like Denzel, wait for another flight.

Important tip!

If your pilot is named *Tully*, go with him.

In the Alaska bush I'd rather have a two hour bladder and three hours of gas than vice versa.

~ Kurt Wien

Ground Control: "421KJ, bear to the left. There's a bad ice slick on the runway on your right.

Pilot: "421KJ, Roger. I have the ice slick in sight, but I don't see the bear yet.

There were three Pilots, a Mexican, an American, and a Japanese pilot. They were taking turns flying over each of their countries. First, they flew over Japan and the Japanese Pilot dropped an apple on his country. The other two ask why he did that and he said "Because I love my country!"

Next, they went to Mexico and the Mexican Pilot drops an orange on his country. Again, the other two asked why he did that, and he said "Because I love my country"

Last, they flew over America and the American Pilot drops a bomb on his country. The other two asked him why he did that and he said "Because I hate my country."

After they each landed in their respective countries, the Japanese guy was walking and he saw a kid crying and asked, "What's the matter? Why are you crying?"

The kid said, "An apple fell out of the sky and hit me in the head. "

Then the Mexican was walking and he saw a kid crying and he asked, "What happened?"

The kid said, "An orange fell out of the sky and hit me in the head. "

Then the American was walking and he saw a kid laughing and he asked, "What are you so happy about?"

And he said "I farted and the building behind me exploded."

What's the difference between God and an Airline Pilot?

God doesn't think He's a pilot

Did you hear about the stupid depressed pilot? He parked his car in the garage, rolled up the windows, and left the motor running on his all-electric car.

And from the pilot during his welcome message: "Delta Airlines is pleased to have some of the best flight attendants in the industry. Unfortunately, none of them are on this flight!"

Never, I repeat never fly with a pilot who needs training wheels.

© 2017 Robert D. Reed

A student became lost during a solo cross-country flight. While attempting to locate the aircraft on radar, ATC asks, "What was your last known position?"

The reply:"When I was number one for takeoff."

I used to dream about being an astronaut. I just never had the grades. Or the physical endurance. Plus I threw up a lot and nobody liked spending a week with me.

~ Philip J. Fry, *Futurama* TV show,
"The Series Has Landed"

Two pilots were sitting in a bar after a long day of flying, and Roger said, "Frank, aren't you going to call your wife. You said you were going to be home at 9. It is already 10:30."

He answered, "No, do you think I want to fight twice?

So a little boy and his mommy are on an airplane. The little boy asks "Mommy, if mommies and daddies can make babies and mommy and daddy doggies can make puppies, then how do mommy and daddy airplanes make babies?"

The mom says "I don't know but go ask the pilot"

The little boy goes to the pilot and asks him his question, and the pilot says "Our Airplanes don't make babies because we're Southwest Airlines and we pull out on time!"

The propeller is just a big fan in front of the plane used to keep the pilot cool. When it stops, you can actually watch the pilot start sweating.

Congrats to *21 Pilots* (Josh Dun, Tyler Joseph, 2017 Grammys, Winners) for their Grammy win; but Fellas, do you know what you started at the airlines? Please apologize!

A JOKE FOR YOU
TO FILL IN THE BLANKS

_____ are on their way from
_____to _____.

_____ says, "I think
that I will throw a hundred-dollar bill out the
window and make someone very excited."

_____ says, "Let's
throw ten $10 bills out the window and make ten
people happy."

_____ very astutely says,
"Wherever we throw the money, it has to be
over _____. They are the only ones
dumb enough to look for money falling from the
sky."

_____ says, "No, we need
to impact more people. Let's throw out a hundred $1 bills and make a hundred people think

_____.

_____ hears about this
preposterous plan and proclaims: "Throw them
all out the window and make the world rejoice/
sane/_____."

Three old timer former turboprop pilots, a little hard of hearing, are talking.

First one says, "Man! It's windy."

Second one says, "NO, it's Thursday."

Third one says, "Me too! Let's go get a drink."

It's better to break ground and head into the wind than to break wind and head into the ground.

A male pilot is a confused soul who talks about women when he's flying, and about flying when he's with a woman.

A ground-school instructor understands piloting the way an astronomer understands the stars.

A pilot walks up to Saint Peter who was standing at the Pearly Gates and says, "My name is Joe. I'm a pilot. I think you have got a place for me."

Saint Peter starts flipping through his book and says, "Ah yes, Joe. Here you are. Take this *golden staff, harp, and silk robe,* and pass through to the right where you will meet the choir you have been assigned."

A minute later, another man walks up. "Hello Saint Peter. My name is Bob and I am a retired pastor. I think you have got a place for me."

Saint Peter starts flipping through his book. "Ah yes, Bob, here you are. Take *this wooden staff, this ukulele, and this cotton robe,* and pass through to the right where you will meet the choir you have been assigned."

Bob says (a little miffed), "Well, alright, I guess... but why did that pilot get all that fancy stuff and I got this plain stuff?"

Saint Peter says, "Well, you see, Bob, we work on the cause-and-effect principle here. While you spent years preaching, most of your congregation was asleep. When Joe was flying, everybody who flew with him was praying."

Chapter Five

MECHANICS

P = The problem logged by the pilot.
S = The solution logged by the mechanic.

✈ P: Left inside main tire almost needs replacement.

S: Almost replaced left inside main tire.

✈ P: Test flight OK, except auto-land very rough.

S: Auto-land not installed on this aircraft.

✈ P: Something loose in cockpit.

S: Something tightened in cockpit.

✈ P: Dead bugs on windshield.

S: Live bugs on backorder.

✈ P: Autopilot in "altitude-hold" mode produces a 200-feet-per-minute descent.

S: Cannot reproduce problem on ground.

✈ P: Evidence of leak on right main landing gear.

S: Evidence removed.

✈ P: DME volume unbelievably loud.

S: DME volume set to more believable level.

✈ P: Friction locks cause throttle levers to stick.

S: That's what they're for!

✈ P: Transponder inoperative.

S: Transponder always inoperative in OFF mode.

✈ P: Suspected crack in windscreen.

S: Suspect you're right.

✈ P: Number 3 engine missing.

S: Engine found on right wing after brief search.

✈ P: Radar hums.
   S: Reprogrammed radar with words.

✈ P: Radar hums.
   S: Reprogrammed radar with words.

✈ P: Funny smell in cockpit.
   S: Pilot told to change cologne.

✈ P: Aircraft handles funny.
   S: Aircraft warned to straighten up, fly right,
      and be serious.

✈ P: Radio switches stick.
   S: Peanut butter no longer served to flight
      crew.

✈ P: Screaming sound in cabin at start-up.
   S: Company accountant deplaned.

✈ P: Aircraft 2,400 lbs over max weight.
   S: Aircraft put on diet of 92 octane.

✈ P: #3 engine knocks at idle.
   S: #3 engine let in for a few beers.

✈ P: #3 engine runs like it's sick.

S: #3 engine diagnosed with hangover.

✈ P: Brakes howl on application.

S: Don't step on 'em so hard!

✈ P: Radio sounds like a squealing pig.

S: Removed pig from radio. BBQ behind hangar tomorrow.

✈ P: First class cabin floor has a squeak.

S: Co-pilot told not to play with toddler toys in cabin anymore.

✈ P: Electrical governor is broke.

S: Paid off governor's debt to Jimmy "The Fish" Galvano.

✈ P: Air conditioning motor makes a loud squeal like my mother-in-law.

S: Recommend divorce.

✈ P: Noise coming from under instrument panel. Sounds like a midget pounding on something with a hammer.

S: Took hammer away from midget.

Bud and Jim were drinking buddies who worked as airplane mechanics in Atlanta. One day the airport was fogged in and they were stuck in the hangar with nothing to do. Bud said, "Man, I wish we had something to drink!"

Jim says, "Me too. Y' know, I've heard you can drink jet fuel and get a buzz. You wanna try it?" So they poured themselves a couple of glasses of high octane hooch and got completely smashed. The next morning Bud woke up surprised at how good he felt; in fact he felt GREAT! NO hangover! NO bad side effects. Nothing! Then the phone rings . . . It's Jim. Jim says, "Hey, how do you feel this morning?"

Bud says, "I feel great. How about you?"

Jim says, "I feel great, too. You don't have a hangover?"

Bud says, "No. That jet fuel is great stuff—no hangover, nothing. We ought to do this more often."

"Yeah, well, there's just one thing . . ."

"What's that?"

"Have you farted yet?"

"No . . ."

"Well, DON'T, 'cause I'm in PHOENIX!

Angels can fly
because they take
themselves lightly.

~ G. K. Chesterton,
Orthodoxy, 1908

Chapter Six

FLIGHT ATTENDANTS

© 2017 Robert D. Reed

From a Southwest Airlines employee: "Welcome aboard Southwest Flight 245 to Tampa. To operate your seat belt, insert the metal tab into the buckle, and pull tight. It works just like every other seat belt; and, if you don't know how to operate one, you probably shouldn't be out in public unsupervised."

Heard on a Southwest Airline flight 'Ladies and gentlemen, if you wish to smoke, the smoking section on this airplane is on the wing and if you can light 'em, you can smoke 'em.'

The pilot says to the flight attendants, "We're going down. We are out of gas and the airport is too far away. Are all the passengers in their seats and buckled in?"

A flight attendant replies, "All are except for Bob Reed, the author of **Flightmares**. He is passing out free copies of his book. He wants to make sure that if people are going to die, they die laughing."

Muhammad Ali: Superman don't need no seat belt.

Flight Attendant: Superman don't need no airplane, either.

> ~ Clifton Fadiman
> The Little, Brown Book of Anecdotes, 1985

An Airline Captain was breaking in a new Flight Attendant. When they arrived in their lay-over city, the captain showed the new Flight Attendant the best place for airline personnel to eat, shop, and stay overnight. The next morning, as the Pilot was preparing the crew for the day's route, he noticed the new Flight Attendant was missing. He knew which room she was in at the hotel and called her up to ask her why she wasn't in the lobby with the others.

She answered the phone, crying, and said, "I can't get out of my room."

"You can't get out of your room?" The captain asked, "Why not?"

She replied, "There are only three doors in here," she sobbed. "One is the bathroom. One is the closet, and one has a sign on it that says 'Do Not Disturb!'"

The Pope really is flying economy, isn't he?

On a Continental Flight with a very "senior" flight attendant crew, the pilot said, "Ladies and gentlemen, we've reached cruising altitude and will be turning down the cabin lights. This is for your comfort and to enhance the appearance of your flight attendants."

Flight Attendants
Get Asked Questions

Question: Where do my suitcases go when I leave them off at check in?

Answer: We have an arrangement with FEDEX. They pick them up and drive them quickly to your landing destination.

Question: Is there a free Coke machine at the back of the plane?

Answer. No, it costs 4 German Marks.

Question: Is the water in the toilets fresh?

Answer: Only once did I taste it and it was.

Question: Where does the crew sleep on long flights?

Answer: Well it varies. Some prefer to nap right in their pilot seats; others prefer the toilet. Some walk around all night until it is their turn to come back to work.

Question: How does the crew get back home after we land?

Answer: They always stay at the destination until a flight returns to their home city. It can take several weeks.

Question: Is there some sort of cargo planes that carry real big people?

Answer: UPS Air carries some of them with packages.

Question: Is it true you allow little children on the plane to keep the crew awake?

Answer: I really am not allowed to answer that.

Question: If we find a girlie magazine in the seat pocket, can we keep it?

Answer: Only if the crew doesn't want it.

Question: Is it true that there is a cyanide capsule sewn into the seat ahead of me that you can use if the plane is in distress?

Answer: Yes.

Question: Where does all the lost luggage go?
Answer: The same place your lost socks go.

"Last one off the plane must clean it."

Chapter Seven

AIRSICK BAGS

Things NOT to do
while using an airsick bag

- ✈ Don't sneeze while using

- ✈ Do not hand the bag to anyone

- ✈ No giggling

- ✈ Use only once

- ✈ No Facebook postings

- ✈ No selfies please

- ✈ Don't ask for more fish

- ✈ Never sit by me

Flightmare's

Honorary Airsick Bag Collector

Photo by nubi magazine

Niek Vermeulen of the Netherlands holds the Guiness World Record for the largest collection of air sickness bags. He has over 6,290 air sickness bags from 1,191 different airlines and as many as 200 countries.

http://www.xtraspace.co.za/blog/articles/
five-of-the-worlds-strangest-collections

Some *Sick* Advice

A trick heard from Ronn Owens, a well-known San Francisco radio host on KGO Radio: If a plane isn't totally full and you want a seat alone, pick up a sick bag and stare into it while folks are boarding. It works every time.

Chapter Eight

AIRLINE FOOD AND DRINKS

Save the peanuts, buy more rivets

© 2017 Robert D. Reed

Charlie Brown, Snoopy, Dilbert, Dogbert, Garfield, Jon Arbuckle, and a whole lot of comic strip characters and their pets were on an airplane flying from Miami to Los Angeles.

In the middle of the flight, the flight attendant gave out food to everyone but Charlie Brown and Snoopy. They asked him why everyone else got some food and they didn't.

The flight attendant said, "Sorry, but we don't serve PEANUTS on this flight."

The strength of the turbulence is directly proportional to the temperature of your coffee.

~ Gunter's Second Law of Air Travel

What kind of chocolate should flight attendants hand out on airplanes?

Plane Chocolate, of course.

It was mealtime during an airline flight. 'Would you like dinner?' the flight attendant asked John, seated in front.

'What are my choices?' Greg asked.

"Yes or no," she replied.

A man went to the airline counter.
The ticket agent asked,
"Sir, do you have reservations?"
He replied, "Reservations?
Of course I have reservations,
but I'm flying anyway."

Chapter Nine

PASSENGERS

I think we've finally figured out how your frequent flier plan works.

If God had really intended men to fly, He'd make it easier to get to the airport.

~ George Winters

Terminal Illness: that is when you are sick and tired of being in an airport.

Flight Reservation Systems decide whether or not you exist. If your information isn't in their database, then you simply don't get to go anywhere.

~ Arthur Miller

Confused Husband: "Why does my wife always get TSA and I don't? I am the one who for years was in the intelligence field with top secret clearances!

Modern air travel would be very enjoyable . . . if I could only learn to enjoy boredom, discomfort and fatigue. Every time I fly and am forced to remove my shoes, I'm grateful Richard Reid is not known as the Underwear Bomber.

~ Douglas Manuel, aerospace executive regards airport security. Reported in *USA Today*, 13 March 2003

Why We Should Appreciate Flying But Don't

There are scary-looking people boarding the plane with us. (Who the hell are all these weirdos?)

Look at everyone trying to get their super large carry on bags in the bins and under their seats.

How about the person who is carrying a super coffee as well as more carry-on pieces than she should be allowed? She has a purse, a computer bag, lunch, a small baby, and a diaper bag. (Gads, just stay home!)

Now look around at the bodies with all that extra weight and the tiny seat they have to squeeze their asses into! Good luck. What will you do if you get the middle seat between two oversized passengers?

How does a self-centered, obnoxious, and rude person find their way to the seat next to me?

Whatever happened to the beliefs in our individual rights to liberty, happiness, and as much room as we want in the overhead bin?

Why is there always someone in the security line cracking jokes to the TSA people and fellow passengers about shoe bombs, hijackers, and the fact that Bin Laden is already dead?

Can you imagine if the airline allowed unlimited use of cell phones and everyone was gabbing at the same time? God, let me out!

Can you imagine if everyone announced on their phone: "Hello! I'm in the plane to Detroit. CAN YOU HEAR ME?"

When you think about flying, it's nuts really. Here you are at about 40,000 feet, screaming along at 700 miles an hour and you're sitting there drinking Diet Pepsi and eating peanuts. It just doesn't make any sense. ~David Letterman

The odds against there being a bomb on a plane are a million to one, and against two bombs a million times a million to one. Next time you fly, cut the odds and take a bomb.

~ Benny Hill

Bring along your CD, MP3 or IPod player and listen to your favorite, soothing music. "Nearer My God to Thee" is not the best choice.

© 2017 Robert D. Reed

Bring along your CD, MP3 or IPod player and listen to your favorite, soothing music such as The Lord's Prayer, Ava Maria and other tunes to remind you there is an afterlife after flying.

Things People Reported Happened on their Flights

Toenail clipper

An anonymous flight attendant said: "I once had a passenger take off his shoes, put his dirty feet on the seat and clip all of his toenails. It was rude; there were toenails flying everywhere. He also left a nice pile of his hacked off heel skin on the seat for someone else to deal with."

Demanding the engines be turned off

One traveler said: "I was flying a red-eye first class from Dubai to New York. I'm sitting there on my phone, and I hear some guy say, 'Excuse me, could you ask the pilot to turn off the left engine, so my son can get some sleep?'"

Urination in the aisle

One passenger even went as far asto drophis trousers in the aisle and urinate on the floor when he couldn't be bothered to wait for the toilet to be free.

Overweight, difficult passenger

Another recurring problem revolves around overweight passengers. One crew member reported that he was faced with an angry overweight passenger who didn't want to sit next to a man of the same size. After telling the man that he could not move seats, he continued to kick up a fuss by leaning out into the aisle. The crew member then proceeded to wake the man up *accidentally* every time he drifted off!

Spilled water

Once a woman spilled a bottle of water on herself and demanded five vodkas and ten blankets as compensation. After being denied, the angry passenger decided to *stomp up to the cockpit* and shout that a flight attendant had punched her.

Drunk passengers

It's no surprise that flight attendants claimed drunk flyers were by far the most challenging passengers to share a flight with. In some cases, intoxicated passengers are arrested upon arrival at their destination.

"In the event of a sudden loss of cabin pressure, masks will descend from the ceiling. Stop screaming, grab the mask, and pull it over your face. If you have a small child traveling with you, secure your mask before assisting with theirs. If you are traveling with more than one small child, pick your favorite."

© 2017 Robert D. Reed

There are only two emotions in a plane: boredom and terror.

~ Orson Welles

A man was caught masturbating on a plane. When he got off the plane, he was charged with *"Hi-jacking."*

Pilot: Have you ever flown in a small plane before?

Passenger: No, I have not.

Pilot: Well, here is some chewing gum. It will help to keep your ears from popping.

Pilot (after the plane landed): Did the gum help?

Passenger: Yep. It worked fine. The only trouble is I can't get the gum out of my ears.

A guy called a budget airline to book a flight. The operator asked: "How many people are traveling?"

"How should I know?" said the man. "It's your plane!"

An airplane encountered some turbulence, it started juddering and rocking noticeably from side to side. The flight crew wheeled out the drinks cart to keep the passengers calm. The attendant asked a business man "Would you like a drink? "Why not?" he replied unkindly "I'll have whatever the pilot's been having.

If black boxes
survive air crashes,
why don't they make
the whole plane
out of that stuff?

~ George Carlin

Chapter Ten

LANDINGS

"There may be 50 ways to leave your lover, but there are only 4 ways out of this airplane"

"Thank you for flying Delta Business Express. We hope you enjoyed giving us the business as much as we enjoyed taking you for a ride."

"Weather at our destination is 50 degrees with some broken clouds, but we'll try to have them fixed before we arrive. Thank you, and remember; nobody loves you, or your money, more than Southwest Airlines."

Your seat cushions can be used for
flotation and, in the event of an emergency
water landing, please paddle to shore
and take them with our compliments.

© 2017 Robert D. Reed

"As you exit the plane, make sure to gather all
of your belongings. Anything left behind will be
distributed evenly among the flight attendant, so
please makes sure it is something we would like
to have. Please do not leave children or spouses."

© 2017 Robert D. Reed

Overheard on an American Airlines flight into Amarillo, Texas, on a particularly windy and bumpy day: During the final approach, the Captain was really having to fight it. After an extremely hard landing, the Flight Attendant said, "Ladies and Gentlemen, welcome to Amarillo. Please remain in your seats with your seat belts fastened while the Captain taxis what's left of our airplane to the gate!"

Part of a flight attendant's arrival announcement: "We'd like to thank you folks for flying with us today. And, the next time you get the insane urge to go blasting through the skies in a pressurized metal tube, we hope you'll think of US Airways."

As the plane landed and was coming to a stop at Ronald Reagan, a lone voice came over the loudspeaker: "Whoa, big fella. WHOA!"

After a particularly rough landing during thunderstorms in Memphis, a flight attendant on a Northwest flight announced, "Please take care when opening the overhead compartments because, after a landing like that, sure as hell everything has shifted."

Heard on Southwest Airlines just after a very hard landing in Salt Lake City: The flight attendant came on the intercom and said, "That was quite a bump, and I know what y'all are thinking. I'm here to tell you it wasn't the airline's fault; it wasn't the pilot's fault; it wasn't the flight attendant's fault; it was the asphalt."

A hard landing doesn't necessarily mean you've been shot down

© 2017 Robert D. Reed

An airline pilot wrote that on this particular flight he had hammered his ship into the runway really hard. The airline had a policy which required the first officer to stand at the door while the passengers exited, smile, and say a few kind words.

"Thanks for flying our airline." He said that, in light of his bad landing, he had a hard time looking the passengers in the eye, thinking that someone would have a smart comment. Finally everyone had gotten off except for a little old lady walking with a cane.

She said, "Sir, do you mind if I ask you a question?"

"Why, no, Ma'am," said the pilot. "What is it?"

The little old lady said, "Did we land, or were we shot down?"

After a real crusher of a landing in Phoenix, the attendant came on the horn, "Ladies and Gentlemen, please remain in your seats until Capt. Crash and the Crew have brought the aircraft to a screeching halt against the gate. And, once the tire smoke has cleared and the warning bells are silenced, we'll open the door and you can pick your way through the wreckage to the terminal."

Both optimists and pessimists contribute to the society. The optimist invents the airplane, the pessimist the parachute.

~ George Bernard Shaw

The only time you have too much fuel is when you're on fire.

On a flight, a guy asked a beautiful lady sitting next to him. "Nice perfume.....which brand is it? I want to gift it to my wife."

Lady replies, "Don't give it to her; some idiot will find an excuse to talk to her!"

Every one already knows the definition of a 'good' landing is one from which you can walk away. But very few know the definition of a 'great landing.' It's one after which you can use the airplane another time.

A man seating on a window seat discovered two engines on fire. He began to holler, "Two engines on fire! Two engines on fire!" The passengers began to panic. Suddenly the pilot ran from the cockpit with a parachute on his back. "Don't worry"! He yelled. I'm going for help!"

Seats on airlines double as floating devices. That is crazy. They should double as parachutes!

Newton's Law states that what goes up, must come down. Our Company Commander's Law states that what goes up and comes down had damn well better be able to go back up again.

~ Sign in the Operations Office of the
187th Assault Helicopter Company,
Tay Ninh, Viet Nam, 1971

The young and not so bright new pilot was learning to fly a helicopter. After two hours of great flying, she crashed.

When asked by crash investigator what happened, she said, "I got cold so I turned off the fan."

Chapter Eleven

DRONES

Home Security

You can send a drone up while you are away from home and get a signal from your home security device that someone is on your front porch. Launch a drone and scare the hell out of them.

OOPS, it's the Watch Tower people! Sorry!

Ever hear of a peeping drone?

Not funny!

I had a drone come up to my bedroom window at night and a voice said, "Please close the drapes."

What will happen when every nut has drone, a gun, and an enemies list? I am buying an anti-drone and installing it on the roof. I dare you to fly over my home!

I am starting a Missing-Drone Department in Washington and hopefully all states will be encouraged to follow through. We cannot have missing packages, children, dogs, groceries, bombs and so on, missing without a clearing house to report missing drones. Sort an Amber Alert system for drones.

Neil says on-line, "Is the Amazon drone dating anyone? I could use a bf with a job."

A drone doesn't care if you come to the door naked.

Pet Watchers

Have a drone programmed to periodically fly around and drop a treat, play a recording of you sweet-talking the pet or scolding it for crapping on the lawn or carpet. (I'll leave it up to you to clean it up later!), or deliver a new playmate for your dog.)

Special Deliveries

Send someone a present delivered by a drone.
Not a missile, however.

Amazon will deliver your orders by drone.
Because having your stuff shot down is cooler
than being stolen from your porch.

Just so you guys know—I'm keeping every
Amazon drone that comes to my home.

CyberMonday will be a national holiday when the
Amazon Air drones take over.

After your first drone arrives, five others will
arrive bearing items we think you might also like.

Then a drone will follow that has a job of taking
selfies of you with the drone.

Sports

Can you see this at opening day of the World Series? A formation of blue drones does a fly over.

Two golfers are talking. "Wouldn't it have been cheaper to buy a new ball than a drone finding your ball?"

I have a pier here where we live. I put crab pots in the river and drones pick them out of the water and deliver them to my house. We take out the crabs that are big enough, refill the empty pots with old chicken, and the drone delivers them back to the same location.

Elderly man in red suit,
white beard,
with 8 hoofed accomplices
suspected in sabotage
of Amazon drone research.

Chapter Twelve

HO-HO-HO

Santa may be out of work because Amazon wants to begin delivery of packages by drones.

~ Gary Varvel (www.garyvarvel.com)

John Cole has Amazon's drone technology
taking over St. Nick's sleigh.

Read more at http://www.wnd.com/2013/12/jeff-bezos-
dispatches-santa/#wga5KisIEzAhOpTK.99

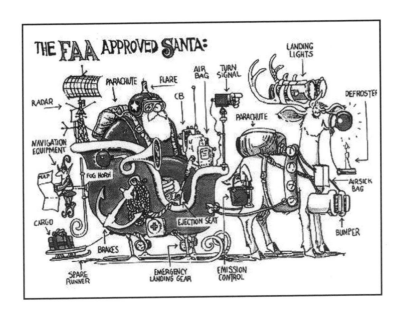

Where does Santa and his reindeer go to get hot chocolate while flying in the sky?

Star-bucks

Never catch snowflakes with your tongue until all the birds have gone south for the winter.

Source: www.jokes4us.com/holidayjokes/christmasjokes/

Hope you enjoyed Flightmares!

MORE FUN BOOKS by
Robert D. Reed Publishers

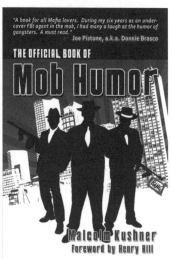

House Calls: How we can heal the world one visit at a time

by Patch Adams, Foreword by Robin Williams
(the actor who played Patch in the movie *PATCH*!)
ISBN: 978-1-885003-18-8, Soft cover, 176 pages,
$11.95 (**SAVE!** Buy 10 books for $89.00; 25 books
for $179.)

The Official Book of Mob Humor

by Malcolm Kushner
ISBN: 978-1-934759-51-6, Soft cover,
192 pages, $9.95

MATH CAN BE FUNNY!

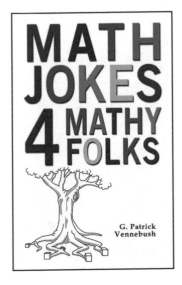 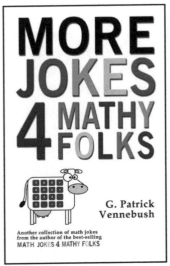

Math Jokes 4 Mathy Folks

by G. Patrick Vennebush
ISBN: 978-1-934759-48-6, Soft cover,
117 pages, $11.95 (SAVE! Buy 10 books for
$89.00; 25 books for $199.)

More Jokes 4 Mathy Folks

Compiled by G. Patrick Vennebush
ISBN: 978-1-944297-18.3, Soft cover,
104 pages, $11.95 (SAVE! Buy 10 books for
$89.00; 25 books for $199.)

Buy both books for $19.95; 10 sets for $179

HUMOROUS and SERIOUS
Educational and Enlightening

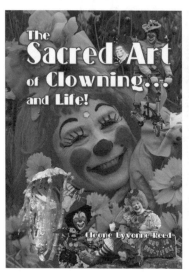

The Sacred Art of Clowning... and Life!

by Cleone Lyvonne Reed
ISBN: 978-1-934759-57-8, Soft cover,
182 pages, $14.95

Teaching School is a Scream!
Confessions of a Career Substitute

by Judy Woods-Knight
ISBN: 978-1-944297-07-7, Soft cover,
150 pages, $12.95
(A must-read for all teachers or wanna-be's.)

Brain Teasers by Kiran Srinivas
ISBN: 978-1-885003-99-7,
Soft cover, 126 pages, $9.95

Get Out of Your Thinking Box: 365 ways to brighten your life & enhance your creativity by Lindsay Collier
ISBN: 978-1-885003-01-3,
Soft cover, 126 pages, $7.95

Die Laughing! Lighthearted Views of a Grave Situation
by Steve Mickle and Rich Hillman
ISBN: 978-1-931741-76-7,
Soft cover, 136 pages, $11.95

Two Books by Mike Clark

Bagel Cartoons

ISBN: 978-1-931741-12-5,
Soft cover, 100 pages, $7.95

Thanks-a-Latte: Not for the Serious Coffee Drinker!

ISBN: 978-1-931741-46-8,
Soft cover, 126 pages, $7.95

Robert D. Reed Publishers
www.rdrpublishers.com

bob@rdrpublishers.com
cleone@rdrpublishers.com
(541) 347-9882

Check out our website for many other
great titles. Write to us or call us.
We'd love to hear from you.